Know Y
Thr
The Four Temperaments

by

Fr. Conrad Hock

NIHIL OBSTAT:
    H. B. Ries
    Censor Librorum

IMPRIMI POTEST:
    Otto Boenki, S.A.C.
    Superior Maior

IMPRIMATUR:
    ✠Samuel Alphonsus Stritch
    Archiepisocopus Milwaukiensis

St. Jerome Library

WWW.STJEROMELIBRARY.ORG

Copyright © 2020 by St. Jerome Library Press
Elkhorn, Wisconsin

No part of this book may be reproduced without written permission from the publisher.

THE FOUR TEMPERAMENTS

FOREWORD

1. Modern educators realize more and more that a well rounded, complete education demands not only training of the intellect but training of the will and of the heart as well. In other words, the formation of character is as important as, if not more important than, the acquisition of knowledge.

2. Intellectual ability is no proof that a man will be able to master the difficulties of life and to adhere to right principles of action in times of distress. Only a strong will and a firm character enable man to stand such trials unshaken. Life is filled with trials; hence the necessity of character formation.

3. The formation of character requires, first of all, the knowledge of an ideal that will "give direction, measure, and value to effort," (Monsignor William J. Kerby) from which the aim and the ways and means of education must be derived. The man who aims at being the perfect gentleman, i.e., the Christian, will of necessity follow other ways and use other means than he whose aim is only to make as much money as possible.

4. It requires also a fair knowledge of **one's self,** of one's powers of **body and soul,** of one's strong and weak points, of one's **assets and defects.** The old Greek saying, "Know yourself!" **holds true also** today.

5. There is no lack of, nor interest in, books on self-improvement. Man is painfully conscious of his many shortcomings and feels a great desire to eliminate unsatisfactory personality traits in order to achieve greater harmony within himself and with his environment.

Such self-knowledge is often offered in learned and high sounding phrases, but more often than not is of little help in daily life. A knowledge of the Four Temperaments, (though sometimes frowned upon by modern psychology) has proved very helpful in meeting and mastering the situations of everyday living. A short but valuable knowledge with practical suggestions is supplied by Conrad Hock: The Four Temperaments. Having been out of print for some years it is now herewith revised, enlarged and offered to the public.

THE PALLOTTINE FATHERS
Milwaukee

CONTENTS

	PAGE
FOREWORD	3

CHAPTER

I. THE FOUR TEMPERAMENTS 7
Introduction. The Four Temperaments in General. How to Determine One's Temperament. The Knowledge of Temperaments Very Important.

II. THE CHOLERIC TEMPERAMENT . . . 16
Character. Dark Sides. Bright Side. Things to be Observed by the Choleric in His Training. Special Considerations in the Training and Treatment.

III. THE SANGUINE TEMPERAMENT . . . 27
Character. Fundamental Disposition. Dark Sides. Bright Sides. Methods of Self-Training. Points of Importance in Dealing with and Educating a Sanguine Person.

IV. THE MELANCHOLIC TEMPERAMENT . . 35
Characteristics. Fundamental Disposition. Peculiarities. Bright Side. Dark Side. Method of Self-Training. Important Points in the Training.

V. THE PHLEGMATIC TEMPERAMENT . . 46
Nature. Fundamental Disposition. Bright Side. Dark Side. Training.

VI. MIXED TEMPERAMENTS 48

VII. QUESTIONNAIRE 50
Character Traits arranged according to Temperaments. Sanguine Temperament. Choleric Temperament. Melancholic Temperament. Phlegmatic Temperament.

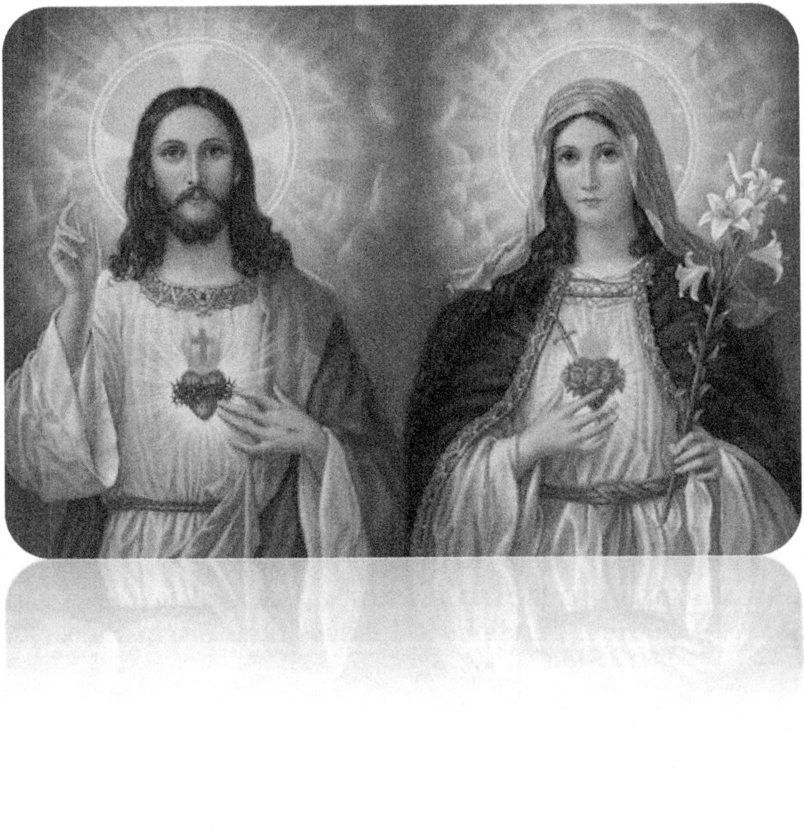

Chapter I
THE FOUR TEMPERAMENTS
Introduction

Socrates, one of the most renowned of the Greek sages, used and taught as an axiom to his hearers: "Know yourself."

One of the most reliable means of learning to know oneself is the study of the temperaments. For if a man is fully cognizant of his temperament, he can learn easily to direct and control himself. If he is able to discern the temperament of others, he can better understand and help them.

I. The Four Temperaments in General

If we consider the reaction of various persons to the same experience, we will find that it is different in every one of them; it may be quick and lasting, or slow but lasting; or it may be quick but of short duration, or slow and of short duration. This manner of reaction, or the different degrees of excitability, is what we call "temperament." There are four temperaments: the **choleric,** the **melancholic,** the **sanguine,** and the **phlegmatic.**

The sanguine temperament is marked by quick but shallow, superficial excitability; the choleric by quick but strong and lasting; the melancholic temperament by slow but deep; the phlegmatic by slow but shallow excitability. The first two are also called extroverts, outgoing; the last two are introverts or reserved.

Temperament, then, is a fundamental disposition of the soul, which manifests itself whenever an impression is made upon the mind, be that impression caused by thought — by thinking about something or by representation through the imagination — or by external stimuli. Knowledge of the temperament of any person supplies the answer to the questions: How does this person deport himself? How does he feel moved to action whenever something impresses him strongly? For instance, how does he react, when he is praised or rebuked, when he is offended, when he feels sympathy for or aversion against somebody? Or, to use another example, how does he act if in a storm, or in a dark forest, or on a dark night the thought of imminent danger comes to him?

On such occasions one may ask the following questions:

1. Is the person under the influence of such impressions, thoughts, or facts, quickly and vehemently excited, or only slowly and superficially?

2. Does the person under such influences feel inclined to act at once, quickly, in order to oppose the impression; or does he feel more inclined to remain calm and to wait?

3. Does the excitement of the soul last for a long time or only for a moment? Does the impression continue, so that at the recollection of such impression the excitement is renewed? Or does he conquer such excitement speedily and easily, so that the remembrance of it does not produce a new excitement?

The replies to these questions direct us to the four temperaments and furnish the key for the understanding of the temperament of each individual.

The choleric person is quickly and vehemently excited by any impression made; he tends to react immediately, and the impression lasts a long time and easily induces new excitement.

The person of sanguine temperament, like the choleric, is quickly and strongly excited by the silghtest impression, and tends to react immediately, but the impression does not last; it soon fades away.

The melancholic individual is at first only slightly excited by any impression received; a reaction does not set in at all or only after some time. But the impression remains deeply rooted, especially if new impressions of the same kind are repeated.

The phlegmatic person is only slightly excited by any impression made upon him; he has scarcely any inclination to react, and the impression vanishes quickly.

In General

The choleric and sanguine temperaments are active, the melancholic and phlegmatic temperaments are passive. The choleric and sanguine show a strong tendency to action; the melancholic and phlegmatic, on the contrary, are inclined to slow movement.

The choleric and melancholic temperaments are of a passionate nature; they shake the very soul and act like an earthquake. The sanguine and phlegmatic are passionless temperaments; they do not lead to great and lasting mental excitement.

II. How to Determine One's Temperament

In order to determine one's temperament, it is not wise to study the bright or dark sides of each temperament and to apply them to oneself; one should first and foremost attempt to answer the three questions mentioned above.

1. Do I react immediately and vehemently or slowly and superficially to a strong impression made upon me?

2. Am I inclined to act at once or to remain calm and to wait?

3. Does the excitement last for a long time or only for a short while?

Another very practical way to determine one's temperament consists in considering one's reactions to offenses, by asking these questions: Can I forgive when offended? Do I bear grudges and resent insults? If one must answer: usually I cannot forget insults, I brood over them; to think of them excites me anew; I can bear a grudge a long time, several days, nay, weeks if somebody has offended me; I try to evade those who have offended me, refuse to speak to them, etc., then, one is either of choleric or melancholic temperament.

If on the contrary the answer is: I do not harbor ill-will; I cannot be angry with anybody for a long time; I forget even actual insults very soon; sometimes I decide to show anger, but I cannot do so, as least not for a long time, at most an hour or two — if such is the answer, then one is either sanguine or phlegmatic.

After having recognized that one is of the choleric or melancholic temperament the following questions should be answered: Am I quickly excited at offenses; do I manifest my resentment by words or action? Do I feel inclined to oppose an insult immediately and retaliate? Or: Do I at offenses received remain calm outwardly in spite of internal excitement? Am I frightened by offenses, disturbed, despondent, so that I do not find the right words nor the courage for a reply, and therefore, remain silent? Does it happen repeatedly that I hardly feel the offense at the moment when I receive it, but a few hours later, or even the following day, feel it so much more keenly? In the first case, the person is choleric; in the second, melancholic.

Upon ascertaining that one's temperament is either sanguine or phlegmatic one must inquire further: Am I suddenly inflamed with anger at offenses received; do I feel inclined to flare up and to act rashly? Or: Do I remain quiet? Indifferent? Am I not easily swayed by my feelings? In the first case we are sanguine, in the second, phlegmatic.

It is very important, and indeed necessary to determine, first of all, one's basic temperament by answering these questions, to be able to refer the various symptoms of the different temperaments to their proper source. Only then can self-knowledge be deepened to a full realization of how far the various light and dark sides of one's temperament are developed, and of the modifications and variations one's predominant temperament may have undergone by mixing with another temperament.

It is usually considered very difficult to recognize one's own temperament or that of another person. Experience, however, teaches that with proper guidance, even persons of moderate education can quite easily learn to know their

In General

own temperament and that of associates and subordinates.

Greater difficulties, however, arise in discovering the temperament in the following instances:

1. **A person is habitually given to sin.** In such cases the sinful passion influences man more than the temperament; for instance, a sanguine person, who by nature is very much inclined to live in peace and harmony with others can become very annoying and cause great trouble by giving way to envy and anger.

2. **A person has progressed very far on the path of perfection.** In such cases the dark sides of the temperament, as they manifest themselves, usually, in ordinary persons, can hardly be noticed at all. Thus, St. Ignatius Loyola, who by nature was passionately choleric, had conquered his passion to such an extent, that externally he appeared to be a man without passions and was often looked upon as a pure phlegmatic. In the sanguine but saintly Francis de Sales, the heat of momentary, irate excitement, proper to his sanguine temperament, was completely subdued, but only at the cost of continual combat for years against his natural disposition.

Saintly people of melancholic temperament never allow their naturally sad, morose, discouraging temperament to show itself, but by a look upon their crucified Lord and Master, Jesus Christ, conquer quickly these unpleasant moods.

3. **A person possesses only slight knowledge of himself.** He neither recognizes his good or evil disposition, nor does he understand the intensity of his own evil inclinations and the degree of his excitability; consequently he will not have a clear idea of his temperament. If anyone tries to assist him to know himself by questioning him, he gives false answers, not intentionally, but simply because he does not know himself. If such persons begin to devote themselves to a more spiritual life, they can usually acquire a fairly reliable diagnosis of their temperament only

after they have practiced meditation and examination of conscience for some length of time.

4. **A person is very nervous.** With such persons the signs of nervousness, as restlessness, irritability, inconstancy of humor and resolution, the inclination to melancholy and discouragement, manifest themselves so forcibly that the symptoms of temperament are more or less obscured. It is especially difficult to discern the temperament of hysterical persons, if the so-called hysterical character is already fully developed.

5. **A person has a so-called mixed temperament.** Mixed temperaments are those in which one temperament predominates while another temperament also manifests itself. It will be a great help in such cases to know the temperaments of the parents of such person. If father and mother are of the same temperament, the children will probably inherit the temperament of the parents. If father and mother are of a choleric temperament, the children will also be choleric. If, however, the father and mother are of different temperaments, the children will inherit the different temperaments. If, for instance, the father is of a choleric temperament and the mother melancholic, the children will be either choleric with a melancholic mixture, or melancholic with a choleric tendency, according to the degree of influence of either of the two parents. In order to learn the predominant temperament, it is absolutely necessary to follow closely the above-mentioned questions concerning the temperaments (page 9). But it also happens, although not so often as many believe, that in one person two temperaments are so mixed that both are equally strong.

In this case it is naturally very hard to judge with which temperament the respective person is to be classified. It is probable, however, that in the course of time, e.g. on occasion of ordeals or difficulties one of the temperaments will manifest itself predominantly.

A very valuable help for the discernment of the mixed,

and especially of the pure, temperaments is the expression of the eye and more or less the manner in which a person walks. The eye of the choleric is resolute, firm, energetic, fiery; the eye of the sanguine is cheerful, friendly, and careless; the eye of the melancholic looks more or less sad and troubled; the eye of the phlegmatic is faint, devoid of expression.

The choleric steps up firmly, resolutely, is more or less always in a hurry; the sanguine is light-footed and quick, his walking is often like dancing; the gait of the melancholic is slow and heavy; that of the phlegmatic is lazy and sluggish.

The expression of the eye rather quickly reveals the choleric temperament (the well-known type of Napoleon, Bismark) and the temperament of the melancholic (perhaps the Curé of Ars). If, from the expression of the eye neither the resoluteness and energy of the choleric nor the gloom of the melancholic can be discerned, it is safe to conclude that a person is either sanguine or phlegmatic. After a little experience, one quite easily determines a person's temperament, even at the first meeting, or even after a casual observation on the street. Physical symptoms of different temperaments, however, such as the shape of the head, complexion, color of the hair, size of the neck, etc., are worthless despite the insistence on such like characteristics frequently found in popular writings.

III. THE KNOWLEDGE OF TEMPERAMENTS VERY IMPORTANT

It may be difficult in many cases to decide upon the temperament of any particular person; still we should not permit ourselves to be discouraged in the attempt to understand our own temperament and that of those persons with whom we live or with whom we come often into contact, for the advantages of such insight are very great. To know the temperaments of our fellow men helps us to understand them better, treat them more correctly, bear with them more patiently. These are evidently advantages for social life which can hardly be appreciated enough.

The Four Temperaments

A choleric person is won by quiet explanation of reasons and motives; whereas by harsh commands he is embittered, hardened, driven to strong-headed resistance. A melancholic person is made suspicious and reticent by a rude word or an unfriendly mien; by continuous kind treatment, on the contrary, he is made pliable, trusting, affectionate. The choleric person can be relied upon, but with a sanguine person we can hardly count even upon his apparently serious promises. Without a knowledge of the temperaments of our fellow men we will treat them often wrongly, to their and to our own disadvantage.

With a knowledge of the temperaments, one bears with fellow men more patiently. If one knows that their defects are the consequence of their temperament, he excuses them more readily and will not so easily be excited or angered by them. He remains quiet, for instance, even if a choleric is severe, sharp-edged, impetuous, or obstinate. And if a melancholic person is slow, hesitating, undecided; if he does not speak much and even if he says awkwardly the little he has to say; or if a sanguine person is very talkative, light-minded, and frivolous; if a phlegmatic cannot be aroused from his usual indifference, he does not become irritated.

It is of the greatest benefit furthermore to recognize fully one's own temperament. Only if one knows it, can he judge correctly himself, his moods, his peculiarities, his past life. An elderly gentleman, of wide experience in the spiritual life, who happened to read the following treatise on temperaments said: "I have never learned to know myself so well, as I find myself depicted in these lines, because nobody dared to tell me the truth so plainly as these lines have done."

If one knows one's own temperament, he can work out his own perfection with greater assurance, because finally the whole effort toward self-perfection consists in the perfection of the good and in the combating of the evil dispositions. Thus the choleric will have to conquer, in the first place, his obstinacy, his anger, his pride; the melancholic, his lack of courage and his dread of suffering; the sanguine, his talkativeness, his inconsistency; the phlegmatic, his sloth, his lack of energy. The person who knows himself will become more humble, realizing that many good traits which he considered to be virtues are merely good dispositions and the natural result of his temperament, rather than acquired virtues. Consequently the choleric will judge more humbly of his strong will, his energy, and his fearlessness; the sanguine of his cheerfulness, of his facility to get along well with difficult persons; the melancholic will judge more humbly about his sympathy for others, about his love for solitude and prayer; the phlegmatic about his good nature and his repose of mind.

The temperament is innate in each person, therefore it cannot be exchanged for another temperament. But man can and must cultivate and perfect the good elements of his temperament and combat and eradicate the evil ones. Every temperament is in itself good and with each one man can do good and work out his salvation. It is, therefore, imprudent and ungrateful to wish to have another temperament. "All the spirits shall praise the Lord" (Ps. 150,6).

All of man's inclinations and peculiarities should be used for the service of the Lord and contribute to His honor and to man's welfare. Persons of various temperaments who live together should learn not to oppose but to support and supplement one another.

Chapter II

THE CHOLERIC TEMPERAMENT [1]

I. Character of the Choleric Temperament

The choleric person is quickly and vehemently excited by any and every influence. Immediately the reaction sets in and the impression remains a long time.

The choleric man is a man of enthusiasm; he is not satisfied with the ordinary, but aspires after great and lofty things. He craves for great success in temporal affairs; he seeks large fortunes, a vast business, an elegant home, a distinguished reputation or a predominant position. He aspires to the highest also in matters spiritual; he is swayed with a consuming fire for holiness; he is filled with a yearning desire to make great sacrifices for God and his neighbor, to lead many souls to heaven.

The natural virtue of the choleric is ambition; his desire to excel and succeed despises the little and vulgar, and aspires to the noble and heroic. In his aspiration for great things the choleric is supported by:

1. **A keen intellect.** The choleric person is not always, but usually endowed with considerable intelligence. He is a man of reason while his imagination and his emotions are poor and stunted.

It is said that Julius Caesar was able to dictate different letters to several secretaries at the same time without losing the line of thought for each dictation.

2. **A strong will.** He is not frightened by difficulties, but in case of obstacles shows his energy so much the more and perseveres also under great difficulties until he has reached his goal. Pusillanimity or despondency the choleric does not know.

---

[1] *If in the following treatise it is said: the choleric or the sanguine person acts thus or thus, it does not mean that he* **must** *act thus, or that he acts* **thus always,** *but that he* **usually** *acts in this manner or has a* **strong tendency** *to act in this manner.*

The Choleric Temperament

Hamilcar of Carthage in North Africa took his son Hannibal to the altar of their god and made him swear eternal hatred for Rome, their implacable enemy. Later, Hannibal assembled a complete army and elephants and led them through Spain, over the Pyrenees, through Southern France and over the Alps into Italy, a feat never equaled before or after, and came very close to conquering and destroying Rome.

3. **Strong passions.** The choleric is very passionate. Whenever the choleric is bent upon carrying out his plans or finds opposition, he is filled with passionate excitement. All dictators, old and new, are proof of this statement.

4. **An oftentimes subconscious impulse to dominate others and make them subservient.** The choleric is made to rule. He feels happy when he is in a position to command, to draw others to him, and to organize large groups.

A very great impediment for the choleric in his yearning for great things, is his imprudent haste. The choleric is immediately and totally absorbed by the aim he has in mind and rushes for his goal with great haste and impetuosity; he considers but too little whether he can really reach his goal.

A high Nazi official told a former chum, (later a priest): "We cannot back out; we have gone too far."

He sees only one road, the one he in his impetuosity has taken without sufficient consideration, and he does not notice that by another road he could reach his goal more easily. If great obstacles meet him he, because of his pride, can hardly make up his mind to turn back, but instead he continues with great obstinacy on the original course. He dashes his head against the wall rather than take notice of the door which is right near and wide open. By this imprudence the choleric wastes a great deal of his energy which could be used to better advantage, and he disgusts his friends, so that finally he stands almost alone and is disliked by most people. He deprives himself of his best successes, even though he will not admit that he himself is the main cause of his failures. He shows the same imprudence in selecting the means for the pursuit of perfection, so that in spite of great efforts he does not acquire it. The choleric can safeguard himself from this danger only by willing and humble submission to a spiritual director.

II. Dark Sides of the Choleric Temperament

1. **Pride** which shows itself in the following instances:

a) The choleric is **full of himself.** He has a great opinion of his good qualities and his successful work and considers himself as something extraordinary and as one called upon to perform great feats. He considers even his very defects as being justified, nay, as something great and worthy of praise; for instance, his pride, his obstinacy, his anger.

The Italian dictator Mussolini had himself called "Il Duce," the Leader. Adolf Hitler followed his example by assuming the title: "Der Fuehrer," The Leader.

b) The choleric is very **stubborn** and **opinionated.** He thinks he is always right, wants to have the last word, tolerates no contradiction, and is never willing to give in.

The Russian dictator Stalin brooked no opposition. A friend of his, during a drinking bout, voiced his disagreement with Stalin's opinion. Fearing for his safety some of his friends approached Stalin the next day to excuse their friend on the ground of having been drunk. Stalin cooly told them that their intervention came too late.

c) The choleric has a great deal of **self-confidence.** He relies too much upon his own knowledge and ability. He refuses the help of others and prefers to work alone, partly because he does not like to ask for help, partly because he believes that he is himself more capable than others and is sure to succeed without the help of others.

Hitler relied on his "hunches" in his war against Russia despite the advice of his generals, convinced that he knew better. He lost the war and everything.

The Choleric Temperament

It is not easy to convince the choleric that he is in need of God's help even in little things. Therefore he dislikes to ask God's help and prefers to combat even strong temptations by his own strength. Because of this self-confidence in spiritual life the choleric often falls into many and grievous sins. This trait is one of the main reasons why so many cholerics do not acquire sanctity in spite of great efforts. They are infected to a great extent with the pride of Lucifer. They act as if perfection and heaven were not in the first place due to grace but to their own efforts.

d) The choleric **despises** his fellow man. To his mind others are ignorant, weak, unskilled, slow, at least when compared with himself. He shows his contempt of his neighbor by despising, mocking, belittling remarks about others and by his proud behavior toward those around him, especially toward his subjects.

A Russian general, asked what he would do if his soldiers came to a mine field, responded that he would order a company of soldiers across it. The fact that he would sacrifice the lives of these soldiers meant nothing to him. (Gen. Eisenhower)

e) The choleric is **domineering** and **inordinately ambitious.** He wants to hold the first place, to be admired by others, to subject others to himself. He belittles, combats, even persecutes by unfair means those who dare to oppose his ambition.

Julius Caesar said that he would rather be the first in the smallest Alpine village than the second in Rome.

Alexander the Great, considered one of the greatest generals of all times, was found by a friend of his one clear night looking at the stars and weeping. Asked why he wept he said: "See those thousands of stars in the sky to be conquered, and I cannot even conquer this world of ours."

f) The choleric **feels deeply hurt** when he is humiliated or put to shame. Even the recollection of his sins fills him with great displeasure because these sins give him a lower opinion of himself. In his disgust over his sins he may even defy God Himself.

2. **Anger.** The choleric is vehemently excited by contradiction, resistance, and personal offenses. This excitement manifests itself in harsh words which may seem very decent and polite as far as phrasing is concerned, but hurt to the core by the tone in which they are spoken. Nobody can hurt his fellow man with a few words more bitterly than a choleric person. Things are made even worse by the fact that the choleric in his angry impetuosity makes false and exaggerated reproaches, and may go so far in his passion, as to misconstrue the intentions and to pervert the words of those who irritated him, thus, blaming with the sharpest of expressions, faults which in reality were not committed at all. By such injustice, which the choleric inflicts in his anger upon his neighbor he can offend and alienate even his best friends.

The choleric may even indulge in furious outbursts of anger. His anger easily degenerates into hatred. Grievous offenses he cannot forget. In his anger and pride he permits himself to be drawn to actions which he knows will be very detrimental to himself and to others; for instance, ruin of his health, his work, his fortune, loss of his position, and complete rupture with intimate friends. By reason of his pride and anger he may totally ignore and cast aside the very plans for the realization of which he has worked for years.

P. Schram says:[2] "The choleric prefers to die rather than to humble himself."

3. **Deceit, disguise,** and **hypocrisy.** As noble and magnanimous as the choleric is by nature, the tendency to pride and self-will may lead him to the lowest of vices, deceit and hypocrisy. He practices deceit, because he is in no way willing to concede that he succumbed to a weakness

---

[2] Theolg. Myst., II. 66.

The Choleric Temperament

and suffered a defeat. He uses hypocrisy, deception, and even outright lies, if he realizes that he cannot carry out his plans by force.

For the true Communist everything that will help his cause is right and just: he makes and breaks treaties and promises; robbery and lies and murder are considered justified if done for the Party and the Cause, without consideration of the cost in human suffering.

4. **Lack of sympathy.** The choleric, as said above, is a man of reason. He has two heads but no heart.

Wars, torture, concentration camps, the death of millions of people meant nothing to modern dictators like Lenin, Hitler, Stalin, Mao Tse tung, and their like.

This lack of human sentiment and sympathy is, in a way, of great advantage to him. He does not find it hard to be deprived of sensible consolations in prayer and to remain a long time in spiritual aridity. Effeminate, sentimental dispositions are repugnant to him; he hates the caresses and sentimentality which arise between intimate friends. False sympathy cannot influence him to neglect his duties or abandon his principles. On the other hand, this lack of sympathy has its great disadvantages. The choleric can be extremely hard, heartless, even cruel in regard to the sufferings of others. He can cold-bloodedly trample upon the welfare of others, if he cannot otherwise reach his goal. Choleric superiors should examine their conscience daily, to discover whether they have not shown a lack of sympathy toward their subjects, especially if these are sickly, less talented, fatigued, or elderly.

III. Bright Side of the Choleric

If the choleric develops his faculties and uses them for good and noble purposes, he may do great things for the honor of God, for the benefit of his fellow men, and for his own temporal and eternal welfare. He is assisted by his sharp intellect, his enthusiasm for the noble and the great, the force and resolution of his will, which shrinks before

The Four Temperaments

no difficulty, and the keen vivacity which influences all his thoughts and plans.

Saul, the persecutor of the infant Church, became Paul, the great Apostle who, as he himself said, did more than any other apostle for the spread of Christianity. He made himself "all things to all men that I might save all." (1. Cor. 9:22) He suffered all kinds of trials and persecution (see 2 Cor. ch. 12) in order to preach Christ, and Him Crucified, and sealed his mission by his martyrdom for the Gospel.

Many Saints, men and women, have done likewise, dedicating their unremitting labor and intense sufferings under severe persecutions to the service of Christ, as is proved by the thousands and thousands of martyrs of years past and of the present, outstanding among them Joseph Cardinal Mindszenty of Hungary.

The choleric may with comparative ease become a saint. The persons canonized, with few exceptions, were choleric or melancholic. The choleric who is able to control his temperament is recollected in prayer, because by his strong will he can banish distractions and especially because by force of his nature, he can with great facility concentrate his attention upon one point. The latter may also be the cause, why the choleric so easily acquires the prayer of simplicity, or as St. Francis calls it, the prayer of recollection. With no other temperament do we find the spirit of contemplation, properly so called, as often as with the choleric. The well-trained choleric is very patient and firm in endurance of physical pains, willing to make sacrifices in sufferings, persevering in acts of penance and interior mortification, magnanimous and noble toward the indigent and conquered, full of aversion against everything ignoble or vulgar. Although pride penetrates the very soul of the choleric in all its fibers and ramifications, so much so that he seems to have only one vice, i.e., pride, which he shows in everything he undertakes, he can, nevertheless, if he earnestly aspires for perfection, easily bear the

The Choleric Temperament

greatest and most degrading humiliations and even seek them. Because the choleric has not a soft but a hard heart, he naturally suffers less from temptation of the flesh and can practice purity with ease. But, if the choleric is voluntarily addicted to the vice of impurity and seeks his satisfaction therein, the outbursts of his passion are terrible and most abominable.

The choleric is very successful also in his professional work. Being of an active temperament, he feels a continual inclination to activity and occupation. He cannot be without work, and he works quickly and diligently. In his enterprises he is persevering and full of courage in spite of obstacles. Without hesitation he can be placed at difficult posts and everything can be entrusted to him. In his speech the choleric is brief and definite; he abhors useless repetitions. This brevity, positiveness, firmness in speech and appearance gives him a great deal of authority especially when engaged in educational work. Choleric teachers have something virile about themselves and do not allow affairs to get beyond their control, as is often the case with slow, irresolute, melancholic persons. A choleric can keep a secret like a grave.

IV. Things to be Observed by the Choleric in His Training

1. A choleric needs high ideals and great thoughts; he must draw them from the word of God by meditation, spiritual reading, sermons, and also from the experience of his own life. There is no need of a multiplicity of such thoughts. For the choleric St. Ignatius it was sufficient to think: All for the greater glory of God; for the choleric St. Francis Xavier: What does it profit a man if he gain the whole world, but suffer the loss of his soul? One good thought which deeply impresses the choleric acts as a miraculous star which leads him, in spite of all obstacles, to the feet of the Redeemer.

2. A choleric must learn day by day and repeatedly to implore God fervently and humbly for His assistance. As

The Four Temperaments

long as he has not learned to beg he will not make big strides on the road to perfection. To him also apply the words of Christ: "Ask and you shall receive." The choleric will make still greater progress if he can humble himself to ask his fellow men, at least his superiors, or his confessor, for instructions and direction.

3. The choleric must above all keep one strong resolution in his mind: I will never seek myself, but on the contrary I will consider myself:

a) An instrument in the hands of God, which He may make use of at His pleasure.

b) A servant of my fellow men, who desires to spend himself for others. He must act according to the words of Christ: "Whosoever will be first among you, shall be the servant of all" (Matt 20:27 or Mark 10:44), or as St. Paul says of himself: He must become all things to all men, in order to save them. (1 Cor. 9:22)

4. The choleric must combat his pride and anger continually. Pride is the misfortune of the choleric, humility his only salvation. Therefore he should make it a point of his particular examination of conscience for years.

5. The choleric must humiliate himself voluntarily in confession, before his superiors, and even before others. Ask God for humiliations and accept them, when inflicted, magnanimously. For a choleric it is better to permit others to humiliate him, than to humiliate himself.

6. He must practice a true and trusting devotion to the humble and meek Heart of Jesus.

V. Special Considerations in the Training and Treatment of the Choleric

Cholerics are capable of great benefit to their family, their surroundings, their parish, or to the state on account of their ability. The choleric is naturally the born and never discouraged leader and organizer. The well-trained choleric apostle indefatigably and without fear seeks souls

The Choleric Temperament

who are in danger; propagates good literature perseveringly, and in spite of many failures labors joyfully for the Catholic press and societies and consequently is of great service to the Church. On the other hand, the choleric can, if he does not control the weak side of his temperament, act as dynamite in private and public and cause great disturbance. For this reason it is necessary to pay special attention to the training of the choleric, which is difficult but fruitful.

1. The choleric should be well instructed so that he can apply his good talents to the best advantage. Otherwise he will in the course of time pursue pet ideas to the neglect of his professional work, or what is worse, he will be very proud and conceited, although in reality he has not cultivated his faculties and is not, in fact, thorough.

Cholerics who are less talented or not sufficiently educated can make very many mistakes, once they are independent or have power to command as superiors. They are likely to make life bitter for those around them, because they insist stubbornly upon the fulfillment of their orders, although they may not fully understand the affairs in question or may have altogether false ideas about them. Such cholerics often act according to the ill-famed motto: **Sic volo, sic jubeo; stat pro ratione voluntas:** Thus I want it, thus I command it; my will is sufficient reason.

2. The choleric must be influenced to accept voluntarily and gladly what is done for the humiliation of his pride and the soothing of his anger. By hard, proud treatment the choleric is not improved, but embittered and hardened; whereas even a very proud choleric can easily be influenced to good by reasonable suggestions and supernatural motives. In the training of cholerics the teacher should never allow himself to be carried away by anger nor should he ever give expression to the determination to "break" the obstinacy of the choleric person. It is absolutely necessary to remain calm and to allow the choleric to "cool off" and then to persuade him to accept guidance in order to correct

his faults and bring out the good in him. In the training of the choleric child one must place high ideas before him; appeal to his good will, his sense of honor, his abhorrence of the vulgar, his temporal and eternal welfare; influence him voluntarily to correct his faults and develop his good qualities. Do not embitter him by humiliating penances, but try to show him the necessity and justice of the punishment inflicted; yet be firm in what you must demand.

Chapter III

THE SANGUINE TEMPERAMENT

I. Character of the Sanguine Temperament

The sanguine person is quickly aroused and vehemently excited by whatever influences him. The reaction follows immediately, but the impression lasts but a short time. Consequently the remembrance of the impression does not easily cause new excitement.

II. Fundamental Disposition

1. **Superficiality.** The sanguine person does not penetrate the depth, the essence of things; he does not embrace the whole, but is satisfied with the superficial and with a part of the whole. Before he has mastered one subject, his interest relaxes because new impressions have already captured his attention. He loves light work which attracts attention, where there is no need of deep thought, or great effort. To be sure, it is hard to convince a sanguine person that he is superficial; on the contrary, he imagines that he has grasped the subject wholly and perfectly.

2. **Instability.** Because the impressions made upon a sanguine person do not last, they are easily followed by others. The consequence is a great instability which must be taken into account by anyone who deals with such persons, if he does not wish to be disappointed.

St. Peter assured our Lord that he was ready to go with Him, even die for Him, only to deny a few hours later that he did even know "this man."

The crowds hailed our Lord with their Hosannas on Palm Sunday but cried: Crucify Him! a few days later.

The sanguine is always changing in his moods; he can quickly pass from tears to laughter and vice versa; he is fickle in his views; today he may defend what he vehemently opposed a week ago; he is unstable in his resolutions. If a new point of view presents itself he may readily upset the plans which he has made previously. This inconsistency often causes people to think that the sanguine person has no character; that he is not guided by principles. The sanguine naturally denies such charges, because he always finds a reason for his changes. He forgets that it is necessary to consider everything well and to look into and investigate everything carefully beforehand, in order not to be captivated by every new idea or mood. He is also inconsistent at his work or entertainment; he loves variety in everything; he resembles a bee which flies from flower to flower; or the child who soon tires of the new toy.

3. **Tendency to the external.** The sanguine does not like to enter into himself, but directs his attention to the external. In this respect he is the very opposite of the melancholic person who is given to introspection, who prefers to be absorbed by deep thoughts and more or less ignores the external. This leaning to the external is shown in the keen interest which the sanguine pays to his own appearance, as well as to that of others; to a beautiful face, to fine and modern clothes, and to good manners. In the sanguine the five senses are especially active, while the choleric uses rather his reason and will and the melancholic his feelings. The sanguine sees everything, hears everything, talks about everything. He is noted for his facility and vivacity of speech, his inexhaustible variety of topics and flow of words which often make him disagreeable to others. The sanguine person in conesquence of his vivacity has an eye for details, an advantageous disposition which is more or less lacking in choleric and melancholic persons.

4. **Optimism.** The sanguine looks at everything from the bright side. He is optimistic, overlooks difficulties, and is always sure of success. If he fails, he does not worry about it too long but consoles himself easily. His vivacity explains his inclination to poke fun at others, to tease them and to play tricks on them. He takes it for granted that others are willing to take such things in good humor and he is very much surprised if they are vexed on account of his mockery or improper jokes.

The Sanguine Temperament

5. **Absence of deep passions.** The passions of the sanguine are quickly excited, but they do not make a deep and lasting impression; they may be compared to a straw fire which flares up suddenly, but just as quickly dies down, while the passions of a choleric are to be compared to a raging, all-devouring conflagration.

This lack of deep passions is of great advantage to the sanguine in spiritual life, insofar as he is usually spared great interior trials and can serve God as a rule with comparative joy and ease. He seems to remain free of the violent passions of the choleric and the pusillanimity and anxiety of the melancholic.

III. Dark Sides of the Sanguine Temperament

1. **Vanity and self-complacency.** The pride of the sanguine person does not manifest itself as inordinate ambition or obstinacy, as it does in the choleric, nor as fear of humiliation, as in the melancholic, but as a strong inclination to vanity and self-complacency. The sanguine person finds a well-nigh childish joy and satisfaction in his outward appearance, in his clothes and work. He loves to behold himself in the mirror. He feels happy when praised and is therefore very susceptible to flattery. By praise and flattery a sanguine person can easily be seduced to perform the most imprudent acts and even shameful sins.

2. **Inclination to flirtation, jealousy, and envy.** The sanguine person is inclined to inordinate intimacy and flirtation, because he lacks deep spirituality and leans to the external and is willing to accept flatteries. However, his love is not deep and changes easily. An otherwise well-trained sanguine would be content with superficial familiarities as tokens of affection, but in consequence of his levity and readiness to yield, as well as on account of his optimistic belief that sin may have no evil consequences, he can be easily led to the most grievous aberrations. A bad woman with a sanguine temperament yields herself to sin without restraint and stifles the voice of conscience easily.

Vanity and tendency to love-affairs lead the sanguine person to jealousy, envy, and to all the petty, mean, and detestable faults against charity, which are usually the consequence of envy. Because he is easily influenced by exterior impressions or feelings of sympathy or antipathy, it is hard for the sanguine person to be impartial and just. Superiors of this temperament often have favorites whom they prefer to others. The sanguine is greatly inclined to flatter those whom he loves.

3. **Cheerfulness and inordinate love of pleasure.** The sanguine person does not like to be alone; he loves company and amusement; he wants to enjoy life. In his amusements such a person can be very frivolous.

4. **Dread of virtues** which require strenuous efforts. Everything which requires the denial of the gratification of the senses is very hard on the sanguine; for instance, to guard the eyes, the ears, the tongue, to keep silence. He does not like to mortify himself by denying himself some favorite food. He is afraid of corporal acts of penance; only the exceptionally virtuous sanguine succeeds in performing works of penance for many years for sins committed in earlier youth. The ordinary sanguine person is inclined to think that with absolution in the sacrament of penance all sins are blotted out and that continued sorrow for them is unnecessary and even injurious.

5. **Other disadvantages of the sanguine temperament:**

a) The decisions of the sanguine person are likely to be wrong, because his inquiry into things is only superficial and partial; also because he does not see difficulties; and finally because, through feelings of sympathy or antipathy he is inclined to partiality.

b) The undertakings of the sanguine fail easily because he always takes success for granted, as a matter of course, and therefore does not give sufficient attention to possible obstacles, because he lacks perseverance, and his interest in things fades quickly.

The Sanguine Temperament

c) The sanguine is unstable in the pursuit of the good. He permits others to lead him and is therefore easily led astray, if he falls into the hands of unscrupulous persons. His enthusiasm is quickly aroused for the good, but it also vanishes quickly. With Peter he readily jumps out of the boat in order to walk on the water, but immediately he is afraid that he may drown. He hastily draws the sword with Peter to defend Jesus, but takes to flight a few minutes later. With Peter he defies the enemies of Jesus, only to deny Him in a short time.

d) Self-knowledge of the sanguine person is deficient because he always caters to the external and is loath to enter into himself, and to give deeper thought to his own actions.

e) The life of prayer of the sanguine suffers from three obstacles: He finds great difficulty in the so-called interior prayer for which a quiet, prolonged reflection is necessary; likewise in meditation, spiritual reading, and examination of conscience. He is easily distracted on account of his ever active senses and his uncontrolled imagination and is thereby prevented from attaining a deep and lasting recollection in God. At prayer a sanguine lays too much stress upon emotion and sensible consolation, and in consequence becomes easily disgusted during spiritual aridity.

IV. Bright Sides of the Sanguine Temperament

1. The sanguine person has many qualities on account of which he fares well with his fellow men and endears himself to them.

a) The sanguine is an extrovert; he readily makes acquaintance with other people, is very communicative, loquacious, and associates easily with strangers.

b) He is friendly in speech and behavior and can pleasantly entertain his fellow men by his interesting narratives and witticisms.

c) He is very pleasant and willing to oblige. He dispenses his acts of kindness not so coldly as a choleric, not so warmly and touchingly as the melancholic, but at least in such a jovial and pleasant way that they are graciously received.

d) He is compassionate whenever a mishap befalls his neighbor and is always ready to cheer him by a friendly remark.

e) He has a remarkable faculty of drawing the attention of his fellow men to their faults without causing immediate and great displeasure. He does not find it hard to correct others. If it is necessary to inform someone of bad news, it is well to assign a person of sanguine temperament for this task.

f) A sanguine is quickly excited by an offense and may show his anger violently and at times imprudently, but as soon as he has given vent to his wrath, he is again pleasant and bears no grudge.

2. The sanguine person has many qualities by which he wins the affection of his superiors.

a) He is pliable and docile. The virtue of obedience, which is generally considered as difficult, is easy for him.

b) He is candid and can easily make known to his superiors his difficulties, the state of his spiritual life, and even disgraceful sins.

c) When punished he hardly ever shows resentment; he is not defiant and obstinate. It is easy for a superior to deal with sanguine subjects, but let him be on his guard! Sanguine subjects are prone to flatter the superior and show a servile attitude; thus quite unintentionally endangering the peace of a community. Choleric and especially melancholic persons do not reveal themselves so easily, because of their greater reserve, and should not be scolded or slighted or neglected by the superiors.

3. The sanguine is not obdurate in evil. He is not stable in doing good things, neither is he consistent in doing evil. Nobody is so easily seduced, but on the other hand, nobody is so easily converted as the sanguine.

The Sanguine Temperament

4. The sanguine does not grieve long over unpleasant happenings. Many things which cause a melancholic person a great deal of anxiety and trouble do not affect the sanguine in the least, because he is an optimist and as such overlooks difficulties and prefers to look at affairs from the sunny side. Even if the sanguine is occasionally exasperated and sad, he soon finds his balance again. His sadness does not last long, but gives way quickly to happiness. This sunny quality of the well-trained sanguine person helps him to find community life, for instance, in institutions, seminaries, convents much easier, and to overcome the difficulties of such life more readily than do choleric or melancholic persons. Sanguine persons can get along well even with persons generally difficult to work with.

V. Method of Self-Training for the Sanguine

1. A sanguine person must give himself to reflection on spiritual as well as temporal affairs. It is especially necessary for him to cultivate those exercises of prayer in which meditation prevails; for instance, morning meditation, spiritual reading, general and particular examination of conscience, meditation on the mysteries of the rosary, and the presence of God. Superficiality is the misfortune, reflection the salvation of the sanguine.

In regard to temporal affairs the sanguine person must continually bear in mind that he cannot do too much thinking about them: he must consider every point; anticipate all possible difficulties; he must not be overconfident, over-optimistic.

2. He must daily practice mortification of the senses, the eyes, ears, tongue, the sense of touch, and guard the palate against overindulging in exquisite foods and drinks.

3. He must absolutely see to it that he be influenced by the good and not by the bad; that he accept counsel and direction. A practical aid against distraction is a strictly regulated life, and in a community the faithful observance of the Rules.

4. Prolonged spiritual aridity is a very salutary trial for him, because his unhealthy sentimentality is thereby cured or purified.

5. He must cultivate his good traits, as charity, obedience, candor, cheerfulness, and sanctify these natural good qualities by supernatural motives. He must continually struggle against those faults to which he is so much inclined by his natural disposition, such as, vanity and self-complacency; love of particular friendships; sentimentality; sensuality; jealousy; levity; superficiality; instability.

VI. Points of Importance in Dealing with and Educating a Sanguine Person

The education of the sanguine person is comparatively easy. He must be looked after; he must be told that he is not allowed to leave his work unfinished. His assertions, resolutions, and promises must not be taken too seriously; he must continually be checked as to whether he has really executed his work carefully. Flatteries must not be accepted from him and especially constant guard must be kept lest any preference be shown him on account of his affable disposition. It must be remembered that the sanguine person will not keep to himself what he is told or what he notices about anyone. It is advisable to think twice before taking a sanguine person into confidence.

In the education of a sanguine child the following points should be observed:

1. The child must be consistently taught to practice self-denial especially by subduing the senses. Perseverance at work and observance of order must be continually insisted upon.

2. The child must be kept under strict supervision and guidance; he must be carefully guarded against bad company, because he can so easily be seduced.

3. Leave to him his cheerfulness and let him have his fun, only guard him against overdoing it.

Chapter IV
THE MELANCHOLIC TEMPERAMENT

I. Characteristics of the Melancholic Temperament

The melancholic person is but feebly excited by whatever acts upon him. The reaction is weak, but this feeble impression remains for a long time and by subsequent similar impressions grows stronger and at last excites the mind so vehemently that it is difficult to eradicate it.

Such impression may be compared to a post, which by repeated strokes is driven deeper and deeper into the ground, so that at last it is hardly possible to pull it out again. This propensity of the melancholic needs special attention. It serves as a key to solve the many riddles in his behavior.

II. Fundamental Disposition of the Melancholic

1. Inclination to reflection. The thinking of the melancholic easily turns into reflection. The thoughts of the melancholic are far-reaching. He dwells with pleasure upon the past and is preoccupied by occurrences of the long ago; he is penetrating; is not satisfied with the superficial, searches for the cause and correlation of things; seeks the laws which affect human life, the principles according to which man should act. His thoughts are of a wide range; he looks ahead into the future; ascends to the eternal. The melancholic is of an extremely soft-hearted disposition. His very thoughts arouse his own sympathy and are accompanied by a mysterious longing. Often they stir him up profoundly, particularly religious reflections or plans which he cherishes; yet he hardly permits his fierce excitement to be noticed outwardly. The untrained melancholic is easily given to brooding and to day-dreaming.

2. Love of retirement. The melancholic does not feel at home among a crowd for any length of time; he loves silence and solitude. Being inclined to introspection he secludes himself from the crowds, forgets his environment, and makes poor use of his senses — eyes, ears, etc. In company he is often distracted, because he is absorbed by his own thoughts. By reason of his lack of observation and his dreaming the melancholic person has many a mishap in his daily life and at his work.

3. **Serious conception of life.** The melancholic looks at life always from the serious side. At the core of his heart there is always a certain sadness, "a weeping of the heart," not because the melancholic is sick or morbid, as many claim, but because he is permeated with a strong longing for an ultimate good (God) and eternity and feels continually hampered by earthly and temporal affairs and impeded in his carvings. The melancholic is a stranger here below and feels homesick for God and eternity.

4. **Inclination to passivity.** The melancholic is a passive temperament. The person possessing such a temperament, therefore, has not the vivacious, quick, progressive, active propensity of the choleric or sanguine, but is slow, pensive, reflective. It is difficult to move him to quick action, since he has a marked inclination to passivity and inactivity. This pensive propensity of the melancholic accounts for his fear of suffering and difficulties as well as for his dread of interior exertion and self-denial.

III. Peculiarities of the Melancholic

1. **He is reserved.** He finds it difficult to form new acquaintances and speaks little among strangers. He reveals his inmost thoughts reluctantly and only to those whom he trusts. He does not easily find the right word to express and describe his sentiments. He yearns often to express himself, because it affords him real relief, to confide the sad, depressing thoughts which burden his heart to a person who sympathizes with him. On the other hand, it requires great exertion on his part to manifest himself, and, when he does so, he goes about it so awkwardly that he does not feel satisfied and finds no rest. Such experiences tend to make the melancholic more reserved. A teacher of melancholic pupils, therefore, must be aware of these peculiarities and must take them into consideration; otherwise he will do a great deal of harm to his charges.

The Melancholic Temperament

Confession is a great burden to the melancholic, while it is comparatively easy to the sanguine. The melancholic wants to manifest himself, but cannot; the choleric can express himself easily, but does not want to.

2. **The melancholic is irresolute.** On account of too many considerations and too much fear of difficulties and of the possibility that his plans or works may fail, the melancholic can hardly reach a decision. He is inclined to defer his decision. What he could do today he postpones for tomorrow, the day after tomorrow, or even for the next week. Then he forgets about it and thus it happens that what he could have done in an hour takes weeks and months. He is never finished. For many a melancholic person it may take a long time to decide about his vocation to the religious life. The melancholic is a man of missed opportunities. While he sees that others have crossed the creek long ago, he still deliberates whether he too should and can jump over it. Because the melancholic discovers many ways by his reflection and has difficulties in deciding which one to take, he easily gives way to others, and does not stubbornly insist on his own opinion.

3. **The melancholic is despondent and without courage.** He is pusillanimous and timid if he is called upon to begin a new work, to execute a disagreeable task, to venture on a new undertaking. He has a strong will coupled with talent and power, but no courage. It has become proverbial therefore: "Throw the melancholic into the water and he will learn to swim." If difficulties in his undertakings are encountered by the melancholic, even if they are only very insignificant, he feels discouraged and is tempted to give up the ship, instead of conquering the obstacle and repairing the ill success by increased effort.

4. **The melancholic is slow and awkward.**

a) He is slow in his thinking. He feels it necessary, first of all, to consider and reconsider everything until he can form a calm and safe judgment.

b) He is slow in his speech. If he is called upon to

answer quickly or to speak without preparation, or if he fears that too much depends on his answer, he becomes restless and does not find the right word and consequently often makes a false and unsatisfactory reply. This slow thinking may be the reason why the melancholic often stutters, leaves his sentences incomplete, uses wrong phrases, or searches for the right expression. He is also slow, not lazy, at his work. He works carefully and reliably, but only if he has ample time and is not pressed. He himself naturally does not believe that he is a slow worker.

5. **The pride of the melancholic has its very peculiar side.** He does not seek honor or recognition; on the contrary, he is loathe to appear in public and to be praised. But he is very much afraid of disgrace and humiliation. He often displays great reserve and thereby gives the impression of modesty and humility; in reality he retires only because he is afraid of being put to shame. He allows others to be preferred to him, even if they are less qualified and capable than himself for the particular work, position, or office, but at the same time he feels slighted because he is being ignored and his talents are not appreciated.

The melancholic person, if he really wishes to become perfect, must pay very close attention to these feelings of resentment and excessive sensitiveness in the face of even small humiliations.

From what has been said so far, it is evident that it is difficult to deal with melancholic persons. Because of their peculiarities they are frequently misjudged and treated wrongly. The melancholic feels keenly and therefore retires and secludes himself. Also, the melancholic has few friends, because few understand him and because he takes few into his confidence.

IV. Bright Side of the Melancholic Temperament

1. The melancholic practices with ease and joy interior prayer. His serious view of life, his love of solitude, and

The Melancholic Temperament

his inclination to reflection are a great help to him in acquiring the interior life of prayer. He has, as it were, a natural inclination to piety. Meditating on the perishable things of this world he thinks of the eternal; sojourning on earth he is attracted to heaven. Many saints were of a melancholic temperament. This temperament causes difficulties at prayer, since the melancholic person easily loses courage in trials and sufferings and consequently lacks confidence in God, in his prayers, and can be very much distracted by pusillanimous and sad thoughts.

2. In communication with God the melancholic finds a deep and indescribable peace.

He, better than anyone else, understands the words of St. Augustine: "You, O Lord, have created us for yourself, and our heart finds no rest, until it rests in You." His heart, so capable of strong affections and lofty sentiments, finds perfect peace in communion with God. This peace of heart he also feels in his sufferings, if he only preserves his confidence in God and his love for the Crucified.

3. The melancholic is often a great benefactor to his fellow men. He guides others to God, is a good counselor in difficulties, and a prudent, trustworthy, and well-meaning superior. He has great sympathy with his fellow men and a keen desire to help them. If the confidence in God supports the melancholic and encourages him to action, he is willing to make great sacrifices for his neighbor and is strong and unshakable in the battle for ideals. Schubert, in his **Psychology,** says of the melancholic nature: "It has been the prevailing mental disposition of the most sublime poets, artists, of the most profound thinkers, the greatest inventors, legislators, and especially of those spiritual giants who at their time made known to their nations the entrance to a higher and blissful world of the Divine, to which they themselves were carried by an insatiable longing."

V. DARK SIDE OF THE MELANCHOLIC TEMPERAMENT

1. The melancholic by committing sin **falls into the most**

terrible distress of mind, because in the depth of his heart he is, more than those of other temperaments, filled with a longing desire for God, with a keen perception of the malice and consequences of sin. The consciousness of being separated from God by mortal sin has a crushing effect upon him. If he falls into grievous sin, it is hard for him to rise again, because confession, in which he is bound to humiliate himself deeply, is so hard for him. He is also in great danger of falling back into sin; because by his continual brooding over the sins committed he causes new temptations to arise. When tempted he indulges in sentimental moods, thus increasing the danger and the strength of temptations. To remain in a state of sin or even occasionally to relapse into sin may cause him a profound and lasting sadness, and rob him gradually of confidence in God and in himself. He says to himself: "I have not the strength to rise again and God does not help me either by His grace, for He does not love me but wants to damn me." This fatal condition can easily assume the proportion of despair.

2. A melancholic person who has no confidence in God and love for the cross falls into **great despondency, inactivity,** and even into **despair.**

If he has confidence in God and love for the Crucified, he is led to God and sanctified more quickly by suffering mishaps, calumniation, unfair treatment, etc. But if these two virtues are lacking, his condition is very dangerous and pitiable. If sufferings, although little in themselves, befall him, the melancholic person, who has no confidence in God and love for Christ, becomes downcast and depressed, ill-humored and sensitive. He does not speak, or he speaks very little, is peevish and disconsolate and keeps apart from his fellow men. Soon he loses courage to continue his work, and interest even in his professional occupation.

He feels that he has nothing but sorrow and grief. Finally this disposition may culminate in actual despondency and despair.

The Melancholic Temperament

3. The melancholic who gives way to sad moods, falls into many **faults against charity** and becomes a real burden to his fellow men.

a) He easily loses confidence in his fellow men, (especially Superiors, Confessors), because of slight defects which he discovers in them, or on account of corrections in small matters.

b) He is vehemently exasperated and provoked by disorder or injustice. The cause of his exasperation is often justifiable, but rarely to the degree felt.

c) He can hardly forgive offenses. The first offense he ignores quite easily. But renewed offenses penetrate deeply into the soul and can hardly be forgotten. Strong aversion easily takes root in his heart against persons from whom he has suffered, or in whom he finds this or that fault. This aversion becomes so strong that he can hardly see these persons without new excitement, that he does not want to speak to them and is exasperated by the very thought of them. Usually this aversion is abandoned only after the melancholic is separated from persons who incurred his displeasure and at times only after months or even years.

d) He is very suspicious. He rarely trusts people and is always afraid that others have a grudge against him. Thus he often and without cause entertains uncharitable and unjust suspicion about his neighbor, conjectures evil intentions, and fears dangers which do not exist at all.

e) He sees everything from the dark side. He is peevish, always draws attention to the serious side of affairs, complains regularly about the perversion of people, bad times, downfall of morals, etc. His motto is: Things grow worse all along. Offenses, mishaps, obstacles he always considers much worse than they really are. The consequence is often excessive sadness, unfounded vexation about others, brooding for weeks and weeks on account of real or imaginary insults. Melancholic persons who give way to this disposition to look at everything through a dark glass, gradually

The Four Temperaments

become pessimists, that is, persons who always expect a bad result; hypochondriacs, that is, persons who complain continually of insignificant ailments and constantly fear grave sickness; misanthropes, that is, persons who suffer from fear and hatred of men.

f) He finds peculiar difficulties in correcting people. As said above he is vehemently excited at the slightest disorder or injustice and feels obliged to correct such disorders, but at the same time he has very little skill or courage in making corrections. He deliberates long on how to express the correction; but when he is about to make it, the words fail him, or he goes about it so carefully, so tenderly and reluctantly that it can hardly be called a correction.

If the melancholic tries to master his timidity, he easily falls into the opposite fault of shouting his correction excitedly, angrily, in unsuited or scolding words, so that again his reproach loses its effect. This difficulty is the besetting cross of melancholic superiors. They are unable to discuss things with others, therefore, they swallow their grief and permit many disorders to creep in, although their conscience recognizes the duty to interfere. Melancholic educators, too, often commit the fault of keeping silent too long about a fault of their charges and when at last they are forced to speak, they do it in such an unfortunate and harsh manner, that the pupils become discouraged and frightened by such admonitions, instead of being encouraged and directed.

VI. Method of Self-Training for the Melancholic Person

1. The melancholic must cultivate great confidence in God and love for suffering, for his spiritual and temporal welfare depend on these two virtues. Confidence in God and love of the Crucified are the two pillars on which he will rest so firmly, that he will not succumb to the most severe trials arising from his temperament. The misfortune of the melancholic consists in refusing to carry his cross; his salvation will be found in the voluntary and joyful

The Melancholic Temperament

bearing of that cross. Therefore, he should meditate often on the Providence of God, and the goodness of the Heavenly Father, who sends sufferings only for our spiritual welfare, and he must practice a fervent devotion to the Passion of Christ and His Sorrowful Mother Mary.

2. He should always, especially during attacks of melancholy, say to himself: "It is not so bad as I imagine. I see things too darkly," or "I am a pessimist."

3. He must from the very beginning resist every feeling of aversion, diffidence, discouragement, or despondency, so that these evil impressions can take no root in the soul.

4. He must keep himself continually occupied, so that he finds no time for brooding. Persevering work will master all.

5. He is bound to cultivate the good side of his temperament and especially his inclination to interior life and his sympathy for suffering fellow men. He must struggle continually against his weaknesses.

6. St. Theresa devotes an entire chapter to the treatment of malicious melancholics. She writes: "Upon close observation you will notice that melancholic persons are especially inclined to have their own way, to say everything that comes into their mind, to watch for the faults of others in order to hide their own and to find peace in that which is according to their own liking." St. Theresa, in this chapter touches upon two points to which the melancholic person must pay special attention. He frequently is much excited, full of disgust and bitterness, because he occupies himself too much with the faults of others, and again because he would like to have everything according to his own will and notion.

He can get into bad humor and discouragement on account of the most insignificant things. If he feels very downcast he should ask himself whether he concerned himself too much about the faults of others. Let other people have their own way! Or whether perhaps things do not go according to his own will. Let him learn the truth of the words of the Imitation (I, 22), "Who is there that has all things according to his will? Neither I nor you, nor any man on earth. There is no man in the world without some trouble or affliction be he king or pope. Who then is the best off? Truly he that is able to suffer something for the love of God."

VII. Important Points in the Training of the Melancholic

In the treatment of the melancholic special attention must be given to the following points:

1. It is necessary to have a sympathetic understanding of the melancholic. In his entire deportment he presents many riddles to those who do not understand the peculiarities of the melancholic temperament. It is necessary, therefore, to study it and at the same time to find out how this temperament manifests itself in each individual. Without this knowledge great mistakes cannot be avoided.

2. It is necessary to gain the confidence of the melancholic person. This is not at all easy and can be done only by giving him a good example in everything and by manifesting an unselfish and sincere love for him. Like an unfolding bud opens to the sun, so the heart of the melancholic person opens to the sunshine of kindness and love.

3. One must always encourage him. Rude reproach, harsh treatment, hardness of heart cast him down and paralyze his efforts. Friendly advice and patience with his slow actions give him courage and vigor. He will show himself very grateful for such kindness.

4. It is well to keep him always busy, but do not overburden him with work.

5. Because melancholics take everything to heart and are very sensitive, they are in great danger of weakening their nerves. It is necessary, therefore, to watch nervous troubles of those entrusted to one's care. Melancholics who suffer a nervous breakdown are in a very bad state and cannot recover very easily.

The Melancholic Temperament

6. In the training of a melancholic child, special care must be taken to be always kind and friendly, to encourage and keep him busy. The child, moreover, must be taught always to pronounce words properly, to use his five senses, and to cultivate piety. Special care must be observed in the punishment of the melancholic child, otherwise obstinacy and excessive reserve may result. Necessary punishment must be given with precaution and great kindness and the slightest appearance of injustice must be carefully avoided.

Chapter V
THE PHLEGMATIC TEMPERAMENT

I. Nature of the Phlegmatic Temperament

The soul or mind of the phlegmatic person is only weakly or not at all touched by impressions. The reaction is feeble or entirely missing. Eventual impressions fade away very soon.

II. Fundamental Disposition of the Phlegmatic Person

1. He has very little interest in whatever goes on about him.

2. He has little inclination to work, but prefers repose and leisure. With him everything proceeds and develops slowly.

III. Bright Side of the Phlegmatic Temperament

1. The phlegmatic works slowly, but perseveringly, if his work does not require much thinking.

2. He is not easily exasperated either by offenses, or by failures or sufferings. He remains composed, thoughtful, deliberate, and has a cold, sober, and practical judgment.

3. He has no intense passions and does not demand much of life.

IV. Dark Side of the Phlegmatic Temperament

1. He is very much inclined to ease, to eating and drinking; is lazy and neglects his duties.

2. He has no ambition, and does not aspire to lofty things, not even in his piety.

V. The Training of Phlegmatic Children

The training of phlegmatic children is very difficult, because external influence has little effect upon them and internal personal motives are lacking. It is necessary to explain everything most minutely to them, and repeat it again and again, so that at least some impression may be made to last, and to accustom them by patience and charity to follow strictly a well-planned rule of life. The

The Phlegmatic Temperament

application of corporal punishment is less dangerous in the education of phlegmatic children; it is much more beneficial to them than to other children, especially to those of choleric or melancholic temperament.

Chapter VI
MIXED TEMPERAMENTS

Most people have a mixed temperament. Some persons, however, have one predominant temperament, for instance, the choleric; but the fundamental characteristics, the light and dark sides of this principal temperament are extenuated or accentuated by the influence of the other temperaments. In general a person is happier if his temperament is not a pure one. The combination smoothes the rough edges of the main temperament. In order to facilitate the recognition of one's own temperament these mixtures of temperaments are herewith mentioned briefly.

1. In the **choleric-sanguine** temperament the excitement is quick, and the reaction also; but the impression is not so lasting as with the pure choleric temperament.

The pride of the choleric is mixed with vanity; the anger and obstinacy are not so strong, but more moderate than in the pure choleric. This is a very happy combination.

2. The **sanguine-choleric** temperament is similar to the choleric-sanguine temperament; only the sanguine characteristics prevail, the choleric ones recede to the background. Excitement and reaction are quick and vehement and the impression does not fade so quickly as with the pure sanguine, even though it does not penetrate so far as with the pure choleric. The sanguine fickleness, superficiality, extroversion, and garrulity are mitigated by the seriousness and stability of the choleric.

3. The **choleric-melancholic** and the **melancholic-choleric** temperaments. In this one, two serious, passionate temperaments are mixed; the pride, obstinacy, and anger of the choleric with the morose, unsocial, reserved temper of the melancholic. Persons who have such a mixture of temperaments must cultivate a great deal of self-control, in order to acquire interior peace and not to become a burden to those with whom they work and live.

4. The **melancholic-sanguine** temperament. In this the impressions are feeble, the reaction is weak, and it does not last as long as with the pure melancholic. The san-

guine gives to the melancholic something flexible, friendly, cheerful. The melancholic persons with a sanguine alloy are those cordial, soft-hearted people who cannot bear to hurt anyone, are quickly touched, but unfortunately also fail where energy and strength are needed. Sanguine persons with a melancholic mixture are similar. Only in this case the sanguine superficiality and inconstancy prevail.

5. The **melancholic-phlegmatic** temperament. People of this type succeed better in community life than the pure melancholic. They lack, more or less, the morose, gloomy, brooding propensity of the melancholic and are happily aided by the quiet apathy of the phlegmatic. Such people do not easily take offense; they can readily bear injuries and are contented and steady laborers.

QUESTIONNAIRE

To help you discover your temperament. Be completely honest in answering the questions. They refer to your natural inclinations rather than your present practice, acquired by effort and self control. The numbers added at the end will give the key to the respective temperament.

Yes No Doubt Temp.

1. Are you quickly excited at offenses and feel inclined to retaliate and oppose an insult immediately?
2. Do you look at life always from the serious side?
3. Do you easily lose confidence in your fellow men?
4. Are you greatly inclined to flatter those whom you love?
5. Are you won by quiet explanation of reasons and motives, but embittered and driven to strong resistance by harsh commands?
6. Do you love company and amusements?
7. Does your thinking easily turn into reflection which may stir you up profoundly, yet not let your excitement be noted outwardly?
8. Are you vehemently provoked by disorder or injustice?
9. Do you have, and show, very little interest in what goes on about you?
10. Do you find it hard to trust people, and are you always afraid that others have a grudge against you?
11. Do you dislike prolonged reflection, and are easily distracted?
12. Do you usually not feel an offense at the moment, but feel it so much more keenly a few hours later, or even the next day?
13. Is it very hard for you to deny yourself some favorite food?
14. Do you easily get angered by an offense, but soon are pleasant again?
15. Are you a person of enthusiasm, i.e., are you not satisfied with the ordinary, but aspire after great and loft things, temporal or spiritual?
16. Are you unwilling to admit a weakness or a defeat, and consequently try to deceive others, even by outright lies?

	Yes	No	Doubt	Temp.

17. Do you love silence and solitude and seclusion from the crowds?
18. Do you easily become jealous, envious, and uncharitable?
19. Do you feel happy when in a position to command?
20. Do you spend much time deliberating, yet reach decisions only with difficulty?
21. Do you like to be flattered?
22. Do you easily complain of insignificant ailments and constantly fear grave sickness?
23. Are you very much inclined to ease, to eating and drinking?
24. Do you feel discouraged by difficulties in your undertakings?
25. Do you find it difficult to form new acquaintances, to speak among strangers, to find the right words to express your sentiments?
26. Do you pay keen interest to your appearance and that of others; to a beautiful face, to fine and modern clothes?
27. Do you persevere under great difficulties, until you reach your goal?
28. Do you become suspicious and reticent by a rude word or an unfriendly mien?
29. Is it very hard to guard your eyes, ears, tongue, and keep silent?
30. Are you loathe to appear in public and to be praised?
31. Do you allow others to be preferred to you, but at the same time feel slighted because you are being ignored?
32. Do you dislike, even hate, caresses and sentimentality?
33. Can you be heartless, even cruel, in regard to the sufferings of others, even trample coldbloodedly upon the welfare of others, if you cannot otherwise reach your goal?
34. Do you have little inclination to work, preferring repose and leisure?
35. Do you lack perseverance; does interest in things fade quickly?
36. Are you inclined to inordinate intimacy and flirtation?
37. Do you lack courage in correcting people; it may show itself in these two forms: a) you go about it so carefully and tenderly that it can

	Yes	No	Doubt	Temp.

hardly be called a correction, or b) you shout your correction excitedly and angrily? ....

38. Do you see everything, hear, and talk about everything? ....
39. Do you love light work which attracts attention, where there is no need of deep thinking or great effort? ....
40. Do you consider yourself as Somebody; as extraordinary, as always right, and not needing the help of others? ....
41. Do you belittle, or by remarks and unfair means even persecute those who dare oppose you? ....
42. Can you quickly pass from tears to laughter? and vice versa? ....
43. Are you easily captivated by every new idea or mood? ....
44. Do you love variety in everything? ....
45. Do you remain composed, thoughtful, deliberate, with a sober and practical judgment, in the face of suffering, failure, offenses? ....
46. Do you like to poke fun at others, tease them, play tricks on them? ....
47. Does a strong aversion easily take root in your heart against persons from whom you have suffered or in whom you find fault, sometimes so strong that you do not want to speak to them or cannot stand the sight of them without new excitement? ....
48. Do you get vehemently excited by contradiction, resistance, and personal offenses, and do you show this excitement in harsh words which may be, and sound like being polite, yet hurt to the core? ....
49. Which of these bad dispositions are yours (check one or two):
    a) obstinacy, anger, pride? ....
    b) sloth, lack of energy? ....
    c) lack of courage, dread of suffering? ....
    d) talkativeness, inconsistency? ....
50. Which of these good traits come natural to you (check one or two):
    a) good nature, repose of mind? ....
    b) Sympathy for others, love for solitude and prayer? ....
    c) strong will, energy, fearlessness, ambition? ....
    d) cheerfulness, facility to get along well with difficult people? ....

*To find the temperament mixture, count up total for each of the four temperaments on a separate piece of paper, then divide them by the following:

choleric: 15, sanguine: 21, melancholic: 20, phlegmatic: 7

Name	Chol %	Sang %	Melan %	Phleg %

Some of the preceding questions refer to two or more temperaments; they are overlapping. The choleric temperament is indicated by the following numbers: 1, 5, 8, 15, 16, 19, 27, 32, 33, 40, 41, 47, 48, 49 a, 50 c.

The sanguine temperament: 4, 6, 11, 13, 14, 20, 21, 24, 26, 29, 34, 35, 36, 38, 39, 42, 43, 44, 46, 49 d, 50 d.

The melancholic temperament: 2, 3, 5, 7, 10, 12, 13, 17, 18, 20, 22, 24, 25, 28, 30, 31, 37, 47, 49 c, 50 b.

The phlegmatic temperament: 9, 23, 34, 35, 45, 49 b, 50 a.

Note: Answer the questions first, honestly, simply, sincerely; then try to classify according to the numbers. The next list will arrange the different characteristics according to each temperament. It will help to get an even better knowledge of one's temperament(s).

Character traits arranged according to temperaments
Sanguine temperament

1. Is self-composed, seldom shows signs of embarrassment, perhaps forward or bold.
2. Eager to express himself before a group; likes to be heard.
3. Prefers group activities; work or play; not easily satisfied with individual projects.
4. Not insistent upon acceptance of his ideas or plans; agrees readily with others' wishes; compliant and yielding.
5. Good in details; prefers activities requiring pep and energy.
6. Impetuous and impulsive; his decisions are often (usually) wrong.
7. Keenly alive to environment, physical and social; likes curiosity.
8. Tends to take success for granted. Is a follower; lacks initiative.
9. Hearty and cordial, even to strangers; forms acquaintanceship easily.
10. Tends to elation of spirit; not given to worry and anxiety; is carefree.
11. Seeks wide and broad range of friendships; is not selective; not exclusive in games.
12. Quick and decisive in movements; pronounced or excessive energy output.
13. Turns from one activity to another in rapid succession; little perseverance.
14. Makes adjustments easily; welcomes changes; makes the best appearance possible.
15. Frank, talkable, sociable, emotions readily expressed; does not stand on ceremony.
16. Frequent fluctuations of mood; tends to frequent alterations of elation and depression.

Choleric temperament

1. Is self-composed; seldom shows embarrassment, is forward or bold.
2. Eager to express himself before a group if he has some purpose in view.
3. Insistent upon the acceptance of his ideas or plans; argumentative and persuasive.
4. Impetuous and impulsive; plunges into situations where forethought would have deterred him.
5. Self-confident and self-reliant; tends to take success for granted.
6. Strong initiative; tends to elation of spirit; seldom gloomy or moody; prefers to lead.
7. Very sensitive and easily hurt; reacts strongly to praise or blame.
8. Not given to worry or anxiety. Seclusive.
9. Quick and decisive in movement; pronounced or excessive energy output.
10. Marked tendency to persevere; does not abandon something readily regardless of success.
11. Emotions not freely or spontaneously expressed, except anger.
12. Makes best appearance possible; perhaps conceited; may use hypocrisy, deceit, disguise.

Melancholic temperament

1. Is self-conscious, easily embarrassed, timid, bashful.
2. Avoids talking before a group; when obliged to he finds it difficult.
3. Prefers to work and play alone. Good in details; careful.
4. Deliberative; slow in making decisions; perhaps overcautious even in minor matters.
5. Lacking in self-confidence and initiative; compliant and yielding.
6. Tends to detachment from environment; reserved and distant except to intimate friends.
7. Tends to depression; frequently moody or gloomy; very sensitive; easily hurt.
8. Does not form acquaintances readily; prefers narrow range of friends; tends to exclude others.
9. Worries over possible misfortune; crosses bridges before coming to them.
10. Secretive; seclusive; shut in; not inclined to speak unless spoken to.
11. Slow in movement; deliberative or perhaps indecisive; moods frequent and constant.

12. Often represents himself at a disadvantage; modest and unassuming.

Phlegmatic temperament

1. Deliberative; slow in making decisions; perhaps overcautious in minor matters.
2. Indifferent to external affairs.
3. Reserved and distant.
4. Slow in movement.
5. Marked tendency to persevere.
6. Constancy of mood.

Printed in Great Britain
by Amazon